ACTION JACKSON

Jan Greenberg and Sandra Jordan

Illustrated by Robert Andrew Parker

ROARING BROOK PRESS

Brookfield, Connecticut

Some of this account is imagined. We don't know if the sequence of events during the months of May and June 1950, when Jackson Pollock painted *Lavender Mist,* was exactly as we have described it. But we do have many firsthand reports about the summer when he made so many of his great paintings—his life in Springs, the way he dressed, the way he talked and walked, and most important, the way he painted—and on those we have based our story.

In the afternoon Jackson Pollock puts on his paint-splattered boots
and walks across the yard.

The wind blows in from Gardiners Bay, bringing the scent of salt marshes and sea lavender. His eyes miss nothing—sunlight on the tree branches, tangled stalks of blackberry bushes, beetles crawling in the grass underfoot.

Caw Caw, the crow he tamed, flies down and lands on his shoulder. His Border collie, Gyp, runs in circles demanding a walk, across the fields and down a country road to the wide, sandy beach. But Jackson turns and keeps going.

The gray weathered barn used to be filled with rusted machinery, old fishing gear, and broken tools. Now it's his art studio, a place for painting.

Some artists put a canvas on an easel or hang it on a wall. Not Jackson. He spreads his out like a sheet, smoothing it flat with his large hands. He wants his paintings to be big, big as the sky out West where he grew up, flat as the marshland behind the house.

Sunlight pokes through cracks in the boards, and flies buzz in the dusty studio air. Sliding doors rattle on their frames. He sits, silent, on the floor, staring at the blank canvas.

Some artists cover the canvas with a base coat of white paint. Not Jackson. He wants the paint to soak into the surface, leaving bare patches peeking through the stains of color. Some painters use oil paint or watercolor. Not Jackson. He'll use ordinary house paint from the hardware store to make this painting.

Some artists paint pictures of flowers or people or landscapes. Not Jackson. He expresses his thoughts and feelings directly on the canvas, calling it "energy and motion made visible."

And still he sits, surrounded by the cans of enamel, brushes stiff with dried paint, knives, sticks, a spatula, and canvases. Waiting.

At last he stands. He chooses a stick and dips it into a can of syrupy paint. Slowly he circles the canvas, stepping around the edges, straddling the corners. Black lines form a tangled web. Now he chooses a brush, working toward the middle. Sprays of color: tan, teal, yellow, and white.

An athlete with a paintbrush, he uses his whole body to make the painting. Layers build with each gesture, new colors emerging, blending, and disappearing into the wet surface. He swoops and leaps like a dancer, paint trailing from a brush that doesn't touch the canvas. "I want to make a longer and longer line. I want to keep it going."

11

Hours go by like minutes. Suddenly he feels exhausted, used up, his inspiration gone. ". . . things get in the way of the flow—like roots blocking a soil line." He puts down the brush and goes into the house to help make supper, his mind filled with thoughts about the wet painting back on the studio floor.

The next afternoon Jackson prowls around the canvas, studying his
work. But he doesn't pick up a brush. Instead he walks the beach past

the sandy marshes and the tall spartina grass that waves in the breeze.
He spends hours sitting on a grassy dune watching the gulls.

In the barn, the layers of paint dry. Almost a week passes before he dips a brush and begins his dance. What is he thinking? Does he see the sunlit beach, the pattern of waves, the interlacing branches of the trees, the lush summer grass outside his studio? "I don't know where my pictures come from, they just come." And the paint flows.

Like the Native American sand painters he saw as a boy out West, he moves around the canvas coaxing the paint into loops and curves. "On the floor I am much more at ease. I can walk round it, work from the four sides, . . . be in the painting." Fireworks splatter of rosy pink. Twisting ropes of white. Spangles of silver. A lavender glow where pink and blue-black meet.

Jackson listens to jazz recordings in the evenings. He likes musicians who improvise, inventing their own melodies as they play. While he paints, the notes spin over and over in his memory. Swish and swish again. The rhythm of the brush matches the rhythm of the music.

If a penny fell out of his pocket, he would leave it. An insect lands
in the wet paint, and there it stays. Nails and tacks become part of
the texture. He caresses the surface with sticky, paint-stained hands.
One, then two . . . handprints across the canvas.

His eyes move up and down, back and forth. With light steps, he follows the sweep of his brush. He stops and a pool of paint pauses. Paint, paint and more paint, dripping, pouring, flinging. "The painting has a life of its own. I try to let it come through."

Again he stops. He climbs a ladder to look down at the whole
canvas. Every muscle aches. But his eyes, his mind, and his heart
know the painting is finished.

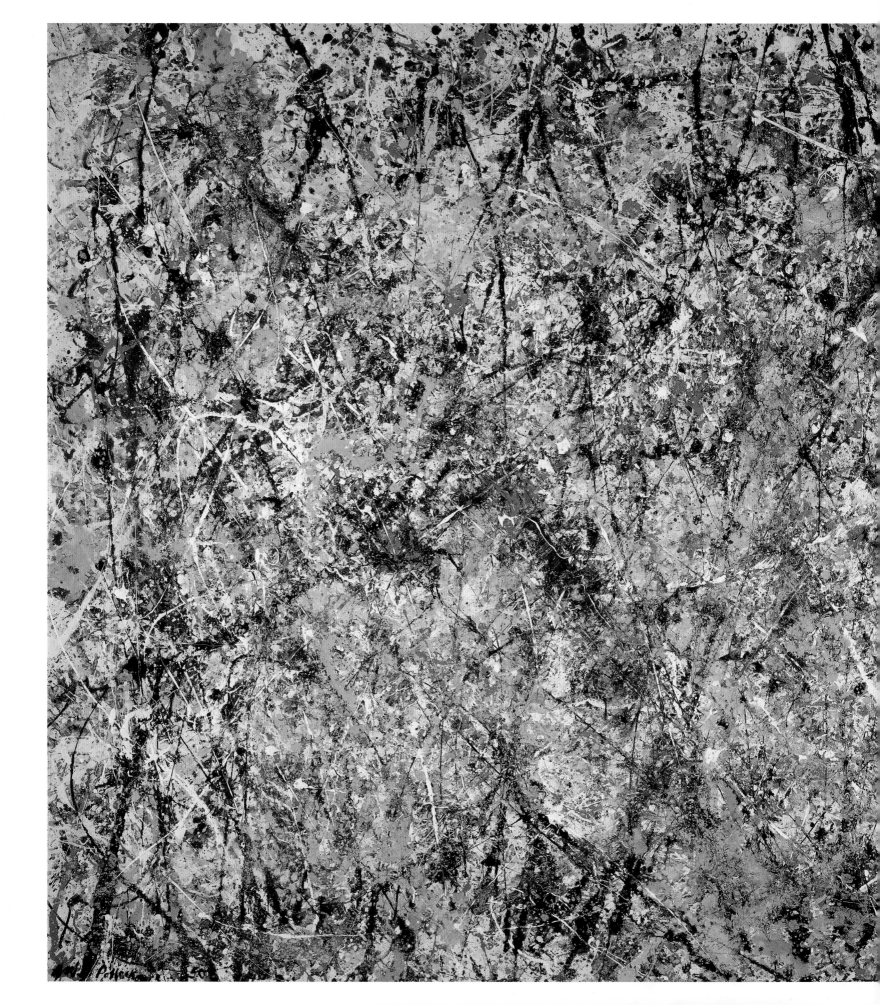

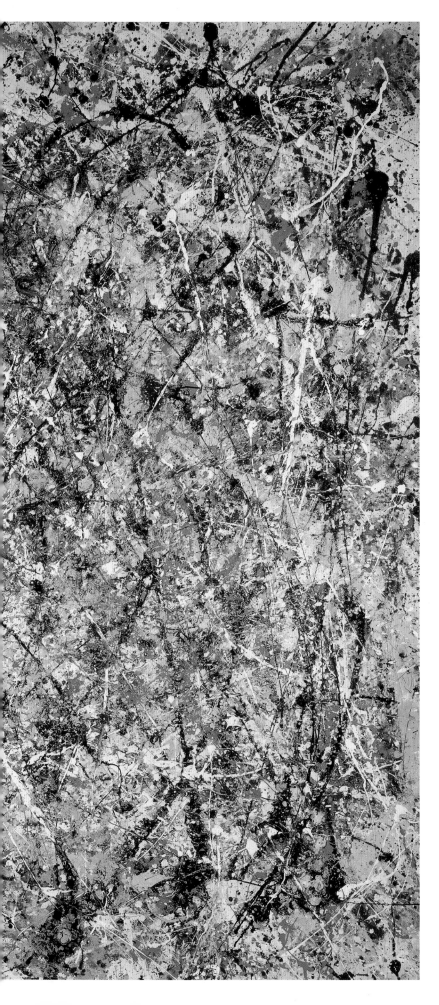

Some people will be shocked when they see what he has created.

Some angry.

Some confused.

Some excited.

Some filled with a happiness they can hardly explain.

But everyone will agree—

Jackson Pollock is doing something original,

painting in a way that no one has ever seen before.

Number One, 1950, (Lavender Mist)
National Gallery of Art,
Washington, DC

Jackson sits, silent, staring at the blank canvas spread on the floor of the barn. Waiting. Soon he will dip his brush in a can of paint, lifting it high in the air to begin again.

Jackson Pollock 1912–1956

Two year old Jackson Pollock.

Thomas Hart Benton.
The Ballad of the Jealous Lover, *1934.*
*Jackson posed for the figure playing
the harmonica.*

Jackson Pollock. The Key, 1946.

Jackson Pollock was a man of few words, a big man with a rough-and-tumble cowboy style. He was born in Cody, Wyoming, the youngest of five brothers. Hard times kept his family on the move to Arizona, then California, always looking for better opportunities. Finally his mother insisted that they settle in Los Angeles, where she hoped a good education would help her sons succeed in life.

In high school Jackson liked English and art. But he was too rebellious to be a good student. He was expelled twice, the second time for throwing punches at the football coach. After that he wouldn't be allowed to graduate, though his art teacher convinced the school to let him come back for his drawing and sculpture classes.

He moved to New York in 1930 to study with the artist Thomas Hart Benton, who did energetic paintings of American life. Benton's use of rhythmic lines to show movement all over the canvas influenced the way Jackson painted. Later, Jackson said that Benton, a realist painter who disapproved of abstract art, was a good artist to react against.

During the Great Depression in the 1930s, after the stock market had crashed and many people had lost their jobs, Jackson worked for a government-sponsored program that was part of the WPA (Works Progress Administration). Artists were hired to paint pictures and murals for government buildings. He didn't earn much money, but he was used to being poor. And it was an exciting time to be part of New York's art community. He began experimenting, painting images from myths and his dreams, and spent hours in museums looking at artworks from Native American and Pacific Rim cultures. In 1941 the Museum of Modern Art invited Navajo medicine men to give demonstrations of their sand painting, which serves a religious and ceremonial function for the tribes. The artists pour colored sand in patterns on the floor, each painting created anew and then destroyed. He studied them closely. Before long his canvases with thick layers of paint veiling the shapes and figures underneath started to attract attention.

In 1945, Jackson married Lee Krasner, who was also a painter. Searching for a quieter life, away from the competitive New York art scene, the couple moved to a Long Island villlage called Springs. Their new home was a rundown rural clapboard house. Lee said, "The house was heated with coal stoves, had no hot water. . . . Not until 1949 when the

Museum of Modern Art had bought a second painting did we call Dick Talmage, the plumber up the road, and have heat and hot water put in."

A small barn on the property was moved and turned into Jackson's studio. There, in the winter of 1947, inspired by the light and the marshy landscape, he spread his canvas on the floor and began doing his most famous paintings—large works called abstractions because they have no recognizable images. He called his paintings "energy and motion made visible."

When these works were first shown in a New York gallery in 1948, they turned the art world upside down. While some reviewers called him the best painter in America, another said his work looked like a plate of baked macaroni. *Life* magazine wrote an article presenting him as a new American rebel. People flocked to see his next exhibition. Because of the way Jackson moved around the canvas, pouring paint from a brush or stick, his artwork was labeled "drip painting" or "action painting," thus the nickname "Action Jackson." He and other abstract painters of his generation are called Abstract Expressionists.

Photo of Jackson as a teenager, taken on a summer surveying trip to the Grand Canyon.

During the summer of 1950, Jackson painted some of his greatest works. After Number 1, 1950 (*Lavender Mist*) was finished, he began work on Number 31, 1950 (*One*). Sometime early that summer a photographer named Hans Namuth received permission from Lee and Jackson to photograph the artist in his studio. For the next few months Namuth took many photographs, including those of Jackson working on the painting that would be called *Autumn Rhythm*. Namuth's still photographs and the twenty-minute film he made form a unique record of the way the artist worked.

By 1951, Jackson was moving away from his so-called drip paintings. Though he still painted in that style occasionally, shapes from nature, animals, and people began to reappear in his work. He was famous now, but he told friends that all the attention made him "feel like a clam without a shell." Jackson struggled with alcoholism and depression for most of his adult life. When he was sober, he painted well, but when he was drinking he felt discouraged and temperamental. His career was cut short by a fatal car crash in 1956. He died at age forty-four. Due to his ground-breaking paintings and those of other Abstract Expressionists, New York became the center of the art world, and a new American art was born.

Jackson photographed by Hans Namuth in 1950.

Notes and sources:

L   *Jackson Pollock*, by Ellen Landau

JP   *To a Violent Grave: An Oral Biography of Jackson Pollock*, ed. Jeffrey Potter

F   *Jackson Pollock: Energy Made Visible*, by B. H. Friedman

N&S   *Jackson Pollock*, by Steven Naifeh & Gregory White Smith

EF   *Pollock*, by Elisabeth Frank

HH   *Such Desperate Joy: Imagining Jackson Pollock*, ed. by Helen Harrison

MOMA   *Jackson Pollock: Interviews, Articles and Reviews*, compiled by MOMA

Page 3. Jackson was not an early riser. His wife, the painter Lee Krasner, said JP often lingered over his coffee for several hours before starting work. *MOMA, p.33.*

Page 4-5. Many sources testify to JP's love of nature and almost mystical feeling for the land, both out West and in Springs. *N&S, pp.516–517.*

Jackson chose the runt of a litter of Border collies and named the dog Gyp, after a dog he had as a boy. *JP, p.168, N&S, p.515.*

Caw Caw was a mischievous wild crow that he tamed. *F, p.121.*

Jackson and his wife Lee Krasner with his model A Ford and the barn/studio in the background.

Page 6-7. The first winter in the house Jackson painted in the upstairs bedroom. Then he cleaned out the old barn on the property which had been stuffed to the rafters with rusty junk. His friends helped him move it from its original location to where it now stands. *N&S, p.518.*

Robert Motherwell, a friend and fellow painter, published a small journal of the arts named *Possibilities* and interviewed Jackson for the first and only issue. Jackson told him, "My painting does not come from the easel . . . . On the floor I am more at ease." Reprinted in: *MOMA, p.18.*

JP occasionally let a few friends he felt comfortable with come into the studio with him. They all mentioned that Jackson not only painted on the floor, but he spent long periods of time sitting there and staring at the canvas. *JP, p.113, MOMA, p.74.*

William Rubin, an art historian, wrote: "Yet Pollock was also at work during the hours he stared at the unfinished canvas as it hung tacked to the wall of the studio or spread on the floor." *MOMA, p.122.*

Lee Krasner describing her husband JP: "About five feet eleven—big boned, heavy. His hands were fantastic, powerful hands . . ." *HH, p.63.*

Jackson gave one radio interview to William Wright, a neighbor from Springs. It was broadcast on a station in Westerly, Rhode Island, in 1951. He talked about feeling "more at home working in a big area." *HH, p.63, MOMA, p.20.*

Page 8-9. In the same interview JP explained why modern artists don't paint pictures of real things. "The modern artist is working with space and time, and expressing his feelings rather than illustrating." *MOMA, p.21.*

After JP died, a poetic statement in his handwriting was found on his desk. It included the lines "Energy and motion made visible—Memories arrested in space." *L, p.182.*

Jackson in another 1950 Namuth photograph.

Page 10-11. Also in the radio interview he said: "The brushes I use are used more as sticks rather than brushes—the brush doesn't touch the surface of the canvas, it's just above." *MOMA, p.21.*

Lee Krasner spoke about his method of painting to B. H. Friedman, who later wrote a book about the life of the artist. "Then using sticks, and hardened or worn-out brushes (which were in effect like sticks), and basting syringes, he'd begin. His control was amazing." *MOMA, p.28.*

Steven Naifeh and Gregory White Smith interviewed many people who knew JP for their long, prize-winning biography of the artist. They give a detailed description of the season in which Jackson painted Number 1, 1950 (*Lavender Mist*). *N&S, pp. 613–614.*

"It's a great drama. The flame of explosion when the paint hits the canvas; the dancelike movements. . . ." *Hans Namuth, quoted in L, p. 182.*

Artist Paul Brach, a friend of JP from East Hampton, asked Jackson why he "threw paint." The artist told him, "I wanted to make a longer line. I wanted to keep it going." *HH, p.277.*

Page 12-13. Lee Krasner said: ". . . he did the baking when he felt like it. He was very fastidious about his baking—marvelous bread, cakes and pies. He also made a great spaghetti sauce." *HH, p. 67.*

Barnett Newman, a fellow artist said: "I've seen him come out of his studio like a wet rag." *N&S, p.5.*

Jackson's good friend Jeffrey Potter took many notes on their conversations. Pollock told him: "When I'm working, working right, I'm in my work so outside things don't matter—if they do, then I've lost it. That happens sometimes, I guess, because things get in the way of the flow—like roots blocking a soil line." *JP, p.128.*

Page 14-15. In the statement in *Possiblities*, Pollock talked about his painting process. "When I am in my painting, I'm not aware of what I'm doing. It is only after a sort of 'get acquainted period' that I see what I have been about." *MOMA, p.18.*

In an interview years after Pollock died, Lee Krasner described what had made her husband happy. "He loved his house, he loved to fool in his garden, he loved to go out and look at the dunes, the gulls." *MOMA, p.34.*

Page 16-17. Jackson Pollock had a few people that he talked to about his painting, and one of them was Clement "Clem" Greenberg, an art critic who was for many years one of his biggest supporters. "I don't know where my pictures come from," was something he said to Clem. *N&S, p.539.*

Jackson Pollock. Male and Female. *1942*

Jackson compared his painting method to that of Native American sand painters. *MOMA, p.18.*

Sand painters are called singers by the Navajo people, and their paintings have a ceremonial and religious purpose. The singer makes the painting by pouring colored sand and earth in ritualized patterns. According to the *Funk & Wagnalls Standard Dictionary of Folklore* (1972), Navajo paintings must be destroyed the same day they are made.

Herbert Matter, a friend and photographer, said: "He worked in his painting completely, naturally, really wanted to be in the painting, and his pouring and dripping from a stick helped him feel that sort of contact. Having his canvas on the floor was all part of this . . . ." *JP, p.129.*

The wet pink and blue-black paint in Number 1, 1950 (*Lavender Mist*) combined and ran together in spots to give the painting a lavender glow. The artist used no actual purple or lavender.

Page 18-19. "Jazz is now and that's for me." Jackson, quoted from Jeffrey Potter, *HH, p.87.*

Betty Parsons had an important gallery for modern painters in New York. After she became Jackson's dealer she saw him paint. "I watched him and he was like a

Jackson moving around the canvas in 1950.

dancer. He had the canvas on the floor with cans of paint around the edges that had sticks in them which he'd seize and—swish and swish again." *JP, p.116.*

Mercedes Matter described watching Jackson paint another painting with handprints (Number 1A, 1948, now in the Museum of Modern Art in New York). She said in the middle of painting he bent down, and his hands covered with 'purplish' pigment . . . began to caress his composition. *L, p.190.*

Page 20. "The painting has a life of its own . . ." is another JP quote from *Possibilities. MOMA, p.18.*

Page 22-23. Usually Jackson gave his finished paintings numbers not names. But he sometimes asked a friend he trusted to make suggestions. Clem Greenberg suggested the title *Lavender Mist. N&S, p.614.*

In 1949, Dorothy Seiberling interviewed Jackson Pollock for an article for *Life* magazine. It began: "Recently a formidably high-brow critic hailed the brooding puzzled looking man . . . as a fine candidate to become the greatest American painter of the 20th Century . . . . Still others condemn his pictures as degenerate and find them as unpalatable as yesterday's macaroni." Reprinted in *MOMA, p.63.*

"The puzzled call them idiotic; the admiring call him a genius." *Vogue* magazine. *HH, p.310.*

Jackson Pollock. Blue Poles. *1952*

Hans Namuth talking about seeing his first Pollock show: "My first reaction was hostile. The paintings seemed disorderly and violent." *HH, pp.260–261.*

"I was in a state of intoxication. I had found myself." Alex Katz, artist, talking about his first reaction to a Pollock show. *HH, p. 149.*

Jackson Pollock, Number 1,1950 (Lavender Mist), *1950 (detail)*

Biography notes

"Mother was instrumental in carting us off to California: she thought the schools would be better for her boys coming along now to high school age." Frank Pollock, in *JP, p.25.*

"let yourself go and paint whatever's in your thoughts." *N&S, p.123.*

The exhibit of Native American art was at MOMA from January until the end of April, 1941.

In an interview in 1981 with Grace Glueck of *The New York Times,* Lee Krasner talked about the primitive living conditions of the house in Springs. *HH, p.81.*

"He thought fame was a huge responsibility. The more successful he got, the more nervous he got." Betty Parsons, one of Jackson's dealers, in *JP, p.114.*

"He talked about being like a clam without a shell." Penny Potter in *JP, p.156.*

Bibliography

Cernuschi, Claude. *Jackson Pollock: Meaning and Significance*. New York: HarperCollins 1992.

Frank, Elisabeth. *Jackson Pollock*. New York: Abbeville Press, 1983.

Friedman, B.H. *Jackson Pollock: Energy Made Visible*. New York: Da Capo Press, 1972.

Harrison, Helen, ed. *Such Desperate Joy: Imagining Jackson Pollock*. New York: Thunder Mouth Press, 2000.

Karmel, Pepe, ed. *Jackson Pollock Interviews, Articles and Reviews*. New York: Museum of Modern Art, 1999.

Landau, Ellen. *Jackson Pollock*. New York: Harry N. Abrams, Inc., 1989.

Naifeh, Steven and Smith, Gregory White. *Jackson Pollock: An American Saga*. New York: Clarkson N. Potter, Inc., 1989.

Potter, Jeffrey. *To a Violent Grave: An Oral Biography of Jackson Pollock*. Wainscott, NY: Pushcart Press, 1985.

Paintings. **Jackson Pollock,** *Number 1, 1950 (Lavender Mist),* **1950,** Ailsa Mellon Bruce Fund, Photograph © 2001 Board of Trustees, National Gallery of Art, Washington, 1950, oil, enamel and aluminum on canvas, 87 x 118" © 2001 The Pollock-Krasner Foundation/Artists Rights Society (ARS), New York. **Thomas Hart Benton,** *The Ballad of the Jealous Lover,* **1934,** egg tempera and oil on canvas, 42 1/2 x 53 1/4", Collection of the Spencer Museum of Art, University of Kansas, Lawrence, KS © T.H. Benton and R.P. Benton Testamentary Trusts/Licensed by VAGA, New York, NY. **Jackson Pollock,** *The Key,* **1946,** Oil on canvas, 59 x 84". The Art Institute of Chicago. Gift of Mr. and Mrs. Edward Morris through exchange. © 2001 The Pollock-Krasner Foundation/Artists Rights Society (ARS), New York. **Jackson Pollock,** *Male and Female,* **1942,** oil on canvas, 73 x 49", Philadelphia Museum of Art, Partial Gift of Mrs. H. Gates Lloyd © 2001 The Pollock-Krasner Foundation/Artists Rights Society (ARS), New York. **Jackson Pollock,** *Blue Poles: Number 11, 1952,* enamel and aluminum paint with glass on canvas, 83" x 16ft., Australian National Gallery, Canberra © 2001 The Pollock-Krasner Foundation/Artists Rights Society (ARS), New York.

Photo Credits. Pages 22-23, Photo by Richard Carafelli © 2002 National Gallery of Art. Page 28, upper left, courtesy of the Pollock-Krasner House and Study Center/Archives of American Art. Page 29, upper right, courtesy of the Pollock-Krasner House and Study Center/Archives of American Art. Lower right, Pollock-Krasner House and Study Center, East Hampton, NY © Estate of Hans Namuth. Page 30, left column, Photo: Wilfrid Zogbaum, courtesy Pollock-Krasner House and Study Center/Archives of American Art. Right column, Pollock-Krasner House and Study Center, East Hampton, NY © Estate of Hans Namuth. Page 31, right column, Pollock-Krasner House and Study Center, East Hampton, NY © Estate of Hans Namuth.

Acknowledgements. It takes many hands to make a book. We are particularly grateful for the boundless help and patience of Helen A. Harrison, Director of he Pollock-Krasner House and Study Center at 830 Fireplace Road in Springs, New York. The Pollock-Krasner House and the studio is open to the public for tours—by appointment from May through October. A special thank you for the thoughtful work of the designer Jennifer Browne. And as ever, heartfelt appreciation for our editor Neal Porter who always is willing to take a leap of faith with us.

A Neal Porter Book   Text copyright © 2002 by Jan Greenberg and Sandra Jordan
Illustrations copyright © 2002 by Robert Andrew Parker   Published by Roaring Brook Press, A division of The Millbrook Press, 2 Old New Milford Road, Brookfield, Connecticut 06804
All rights reserved
Library of Congress Cataloging-in-Publication Data   Greenberg, Jan   Action Jackson / by Jan Greenberg & Sandra Jordan ; illustrated by Robert Andrew Parker.—1st ed.   p. cm.
Summary: Imagines Jackson Pollock at work during the creation of one of his paint-swirled and splattered canvasses.   Includes bibliographical references.   1. Pollock, Jackson, 1912–1956—Juvenile literature.   [1. Pollock, Jackson, 1912–1956.   2. Artists.]   I. Jordan, Sandra.   II. Parker, Robert Andrew, ill.   III. Title   ND237.P73 G74 2003   759.13—dc21
2002006211
ISBN 0-7613-1682-5 (trade)   10 9 8 7 6 5 4 3 2 1
ISBN 0-7613-2770-3 (library binding)   10 9 8 7 6 5 4 3 2 1
Printed in Hong Kong   Book design by Jennifer Browne   First Edition